BREAKING
THE RULES

Meditations and Prayers
by
Eddie Askew

By the same author:

A Silence and A Shouting
Disguises of Love
Many Voices One Voice
No Strange Land
Facing the Storm

Published 1992

ISBN 0 902731 33 5

Printed by Stanley L. Hunt (Printers) Ltd, Rushden, Northants

To Jessamy Louisa Hawke,
sister to Sam.
The future is yours.

Watercolour paintings by the author

Foreword

Dear Eddie Askew

Forgive me if I sound like a fan but my foreword to your book comes as a letter of thanks. I owe so much to you, and I want you to know how grateful I am for your work, both your words and your paintings. You have helped to open my eyes and my mind, and expanded and enriched my whole experience of God's love.

I have read all your books and they have ministered to me quite wonderfully. They have spoken to me in a candid, forthright manner, in a voice that is both wise and gentle. They have comforted, uplifted, taught, and encouraged me, yet they have never pulled any punches. You don't deal in whitewash.

Speaking especially of this, your latest book, *Breaking the Rules*, it brought me face to face with many personal doubts and weaknesses. I was confronted with an uneasy conscience and the turmoil of my shortcomings. Yet you didn't abandon me, confused, and somewhat ashamed. Oh no! That is not your way, and for this I am truly grateful.

Thank you Eddie for taking me firmly by the hand and leading me along new pathways of thought and insight into a richer knowledge and understanding of my life in Christ.

Yours in His Love,

Wendy Craig

"Norfolk Boatyard"

John 4:4-10

WHEN Jesus asked the Samaritan woman for a drink of water, he was shattering convention. Creating a storm in a water cup. Jews and Samaritans didn't mix. Jewish men never talked to women in public, and this particular woman wasn't likely to be received in the best circles, not with her reputation.

But Jesus was never inhibited by convention. Not when he saw human need. Somehow he recognized a human being whose relationships were in a mess. Someone going about the routine of ordinary life, but whose life below the surface was dislocated.

To reach her, he broke the rules, opened doors locked by centuries of tradition.

Even she found it hard to accept at first. She hid behind the common prejudice. She misunderstood. She prevaricated by changing the subject, trying to divert Jesus' attention. She didn't want to face herself as she really was. As Jesus saw her. Eventually, she did and, in facing herself, found the Christ.

It's easy to leave it there, simply to see Jesus as the one who breaks the barriers. But there was a message here, a challenge, for the disciples. It was their business too, to break barriers. And beyond them, he's speaking to the orthodox. "Your life isn't in rules and regulations. It's in relationships. Not in law, but in loving."

Lord, take it easy, please.
Slow down. I can't catch up with you.
Can't find the courage to ignore convention.
Break the mould.

The only thing that holds my life together
is the rules I make.
That's how I know just where I am,
safe in a shaky scaffolding
of do-it-yourself certainty.
Built, bit by bit,
from a prepacked kit of orthodoxy.
Individually designed, they say,
but made to sell in thousands.
Market researched. Acceptable to all.
Matching the decor,
and coming with a lifelong guarantee
against reality breaking in.

I know just whom to like,
whom to invite to dinner, who's acceptable.
And who is better kept at arm's length.

And seeing you behave
as though the rules don't matter,
frightens me.
Makes me tremble,
watching you undo the bolts
that dislocate the framework of my life.
Leaving the house I've built
vulnerable to the first wolf that comes along.

And others feel just as uncertain, Lord,
I wish you'd realize that.
They're happier, too,
if they are able to predict
just what you'll do or say.
More sensible all round.
Of course there'll always be some folk outside,
excluded by my rules.
Unfortunate. But then, that's life.

And, suddenly, I notice, with unease,
you standing with them,
outside the boundary wire of my concern.
Not asking that they be admitted to my world,

but offering me the chance
to leave my warm cocoon,
thermostatically controlled by selfishness,
and take my place with them,
and you.
At risk in real relationships,
where love, not law, defines what I should do.

"Winter Sunshine"

Luke 19:1-10

THE "righteous" were appalled when they saw Jesus making friends with Zaccheus. "A rabbi and a tax collector? Shocking." Tax collectors weren't accepted in polite Jewish society. They were stereotyped as dishonest, anti-social tools of an alien government.

Jesus didn't let that stop him. Here was a man who'd taken some trouble to see him, whatever his motives may have been. And Zaccheus was moved enough by the experience to acknowledge the dishonesty of his lifestyle, and set about rearranging it.

The words Jesus speaks are significant. "Today salvation has come to this house," he says. There're some obvious lessons: that no one, whatever his past, is beyond Jesus' reach and compassion, and that he'll never let human rules or custom keep him from people who need him.

But to me the important thing is the word *today*. "Salvation has come today," says Jesus. It begins now. Sometimes we allow the future to supplant the present. We take God's promises as something to be fulfilled in some distant time we can't see very clearly, and think about only hazily.

Today's problems take all our attention. And when the world looks and feels a grim place, we back off and dream about a wonderful time ahead.

But life has to be lived now, and Jesus tells us that the salvation he offers is for now. The fullness of it may lie ahead, but we can taste it, experience it, live it, today. Jesus didn't say to Zaccheus, "If you're good, you'll get your reward later." He said, "Give your life to me, and I'll turn it around now." His blessings start today.

So easy, Lord, to sit and dream.
To bask, a lizard on a rock,
in the warmth of future hopes.
Eyes alert against a sudden onrush of reality.
Ready to skitter swiftly into shelter
against the shadow swoop of present problems.

But Lord, to build my life
on future hopes, however bright,
does little justice to myself or you.
It's now that matters,
both to you and me.
The present moment is the only one
of which I'm sure.
And if I am to live for you,
it's now that counts.
Not promises of future faithfulness,
whether mine or yours.

If Zaccheus, standing there,
had said, "Just give me time,
I'll change my life tomorrow,"
I have a feeling Jesus might have turned away,
a hint of sorrow in his eyes,
at chances missed.
Another weak excuse,
like those I make at every turn.
Today, you say.
Today, you ask,
and stand and wait for my response.

And that's sometimes made awkward
by the company you keep.
Respectability doesn't seem to be
one of the main planks of your policy.
Good taste seems not to matter very much,
and social status doesn't count at all.
You ask for nothing but the urge to change.
Not easy, Lord, however hard I try.

But lift your eyes and look at me.
Beckon me down from the branches of my hesitation.
Invite yourself into my life.
And help me start, today,
to live in your salvation.

Matthew 5:16

THE day I realized that God doesn't keep count of the meetings we attend was a milestone. I found it very liberating, almost frighteningly so.

Somehow, we seem to attach so much importance to meetings. A full diary of Christian events tempts us to a glow of self-righteous satisfaction. Tony Hancock, the comedian, once parodied this attitude by saying that he kept a record of all the small gifts he'd given to charity, and that one day he'd show it to God, saying, "There you are, Lord, add that lot up." I don't think it works that way.

I don't want to encourage the individualism of those Christians who assume, mistakenly, that they can do everything on their own as long as they have a personal relationship with Jesus, and that worship and prayer with other Christians have no significance. It's important for us to meet together for fellowship and encouragement. We need to know, and to show, that we're functioning parts of the body of Christ, and we can only do that from within the body.

But there's danger in equating our Christian status, if there is such a thing, and our service, with the time we spend at church. It's so easy to assume that we should attend everything the local church does, and to develop feelings of guilt if we take time off to do something else. It's also easy to assume that others should do the same, and to make them feel guilty if they're not there!

I don't believe that's right. Part of our responsibility is to be a Christian presence in the world, not to spend so much time at church that we rarely have time for non-Christian friends and neighbours. We need to know what's happening in the world outside, and to be part of it.

Jesus appears to have been a regular attender at synagogue, but, thank God, he spent most of his time in town and village, moving amongst the people who needed his compassion.

In the parable beginning in Matthew 25:31, Jesus gives his criteria for judgement. They're all about service, about the way we live out the gospel in relationship to other people.

It may be an over-simplification, but perhaps if we spent more time being active Christians outside the church, the church might be fuller anyway, with people who had been helped to see its relevance to ordinary life.

Lord, I find it hard
to sort my feelings out.
So easy to be critical of those
who fill their lives and diaries,
and look to me to do the same.
Put pressure on,
expect me to conform.
"You weren't at church on Sunday night,"
they say, "You missed a treat."
Perhaps I did.
The guilt machinery's in action
once again.

The disapproving attitudes
carefully, although not quite, disguised
in patient, disappointed, smiles.
Suggesting, unless I'm getting paranoid,
and that's a possibility,
that I'm not one of them.
If they still gave a prize
for regular attendance
I'd lose out.
My name not called.

The trouble is, I recognize the faithfulness
of those who make the wheels go round,
who oil the cogs, and organize the calendar,
who fill the chairs when speakers are invited.
We need them, Lord,
but what I'm trying to say and finding hard,
is that I feel a danger
in equating this
with what you'd have us do.

Your message seems to be
that water in a loving cup,
hands held in sympathy,
mean more than all the meetings in the world.
That simple acts of daily kindness
move mountains more than meetings do.
Change more lives,
and make love real.

Lord, let me find a balance.

Psalm 139:1-10

P.D. JAMES writes the best detective stories I know. Actually, that comment is less than fair to her. She writes fine novels, full of deep observation of people and their ways, and crime just happens to be the focus for her stories.

In "The Black Tower", a ten-year-old boy is talking to an old priest. The priest is sitting at his desk, his diary in front of him.

"It's just an ordinary diary, then?" asks the boy. "It isn't about your spiritual life?"

"This is the spiritual life," the priest answers gently, "the ordinary things one does from hour to hour."

Some of us spend so much time and energy trying to be "spiritual". Choosing our words, our attitudes, with care. We see it in the pulpit at times. Preachers who adopt a tone of voice, even a body language, that's strained and artificial. The effect's often colourless and bland and, dare I say it, plain boring.

It's as though we daren't be ourselves; as though the only way to please God was to lose identity, to become production line Christians, all in the same mould.

If we do this we're also in danger of trying to squeeze God out of "ordinary" life, as though there were bits of it he wasn't supposed to be in. Pigeonholing doesn't work. God has to be in everything we do, or he'll end up being in nothing.

The "spiritual life" is our ordinary life, lived with Jesus. It's not a separate entity, a front parlour we keep for special occasions. It's our day to day attitudes and actions, lived out in love. I heard a Christian say recently, "God's not just in prayer meetings and conventions, but in chips and peas." He connects with life as we know it.

The most "spiritual" people I've met, in the sense of being close to God, and living with him, show a worldly awareness that means they are in touch with life as it really is. And, because of that, are competent and effective in the way they live it.

Lord, give me the courage
to be myself today.
To live life as it comes,
welcoming it,
and saying yes to everything.

You made me, Lord,
and made me human,
so being human can't be bad.
Nothing to be ashamed of.
And if you made me different
from everybody else,
it has to be because
you want me different,
and there must be, in me,
something you want the world to see.
Something that only I can give,
some colour to enrich life's palette.

But, sometimes,
caution mixes all the colours into grey,
mutes them to monochrome.
I narrow my mind,
conform to some safe picture of respectability,
endlessly repeated,
leaving me faded, dull.

Lord, teach me to live today.
Help me to see
that love and holiness have dirty feet
through dancing joyfully about the earth,
hands joined in yours.
That life with you is whole, and holy.
That everything I do
can bear your imprint,
can be coloured in love.

Teach me that fear is for the Pharisees,
not for the free.
And I am free in you
to paint my picture
as I will.
Knowing that however individually
my brush may paint,
as long as it be true,
you will be satisfied.

Matthew 13:44-46

THE community of Taizé, in France, draws people from all over the world, to worship together in an environment wider than their own different traditions. Its music has enriched Christians from many countries. It has been, and is, a place where many people have begun to find themselves, and also begun to find God. Or should that be the other way round? Really, I believe the two go together.

Brother Roger, the founder and leader of the community, began it during the Second World War as a centre for reconciliation. Recently, discussing the many thousands of visitors each year, he was asked, "What do you wish, above all, that they take back with them?"

He answered, "That they continue searching throughout their lives."

It's a wise comment. Sometimes, when we believe we've "found" God, we think the search is over. We think we've grasped the truth, and have all we need to know. We've arrived. Indeed we have — but we've arrived at the starting point of our journey, not at the destination.

The story of the pearl tells us that the kingdom is more valuable than anything we possess. But it's a mistake to think that, once we're part of the kingdom, we can sit back and admire it. We don't possess it, it possesses us.

The time when we begin to grasp the reality of God-with-us, in Jesus, is a beginning, not an ending. It's the beginning of an exploration that takes us ever further into God, ever deeper into ourselves.

The truth, which is God, and our relationship with him, is too rich to measure, too big to encompass, too profound to fathom. Indeed, when the search is over, it's only just begun.

Lord, it can be so uncomfortable, living with you.
I'd like to hold you tight,
my treasure, locked up, or buried in a field.
I'd feel secure, and certain,
with you to call on,
when I needed you.
Rub the lamp and you'd appear, on time, on tap.
Predictable.

But Lord, there's nothing but frustration
when I try to live like that.
I base my thoughts on self-created certainties.
Draw my own blueprint and try to build you in.
But you don't fit, and bits stick out.
The pattern isn't neat and tidy.
Each time I grasp an odd end of your truth
and try to tuck it in,
something falls out the other side.

I catch a glimpse of you.
A wild, fast moving shimmer of light
and, with trembling fingers, try to cage it.
But, lightning-quick, you slip away, smiling.
Beckoning me into chase.
Leading me to new horizons,
unimagined, strange and beautiful.
It's frightening at times, unsettling.

Lord, you're not an easy-going God.
I'd like to meet you by the fire
on a wet evening.
Armchaired and slippered, glass in hand.
But that's not how you work.
Come the wet evening,
and you'll be dancing in the street.
Singing in the rain. Inviting me out.
Telling me there's more to life than comfort.
That simple certainties are at best
a leaky umbrella.

There's more to you than I can ever fully know.
I'd rather sit and watch it on TV,
the story line complete and edited.
But I'm called out to make the programme.
The reassurance is
that while my search goes on,
you're sharing it with me.

*Living with you may not be comfortable, Lord,
but the adventure, to say the least,
is always interesting.*

"Edge of the Wood"

Isaiah 53:3-6

SOME peasant women in Nicaragua were discussing the Nativity scene set up in church. One said, "Mary wouldn't have been wearing those beautiful blue and white clothes. She'd have been dressed like the poor, like us." Another said, "And she had rough hands like ours . . ."

The birth of my new granddaughter reminded me of the softness of a baby's skin. I imagined Mary's hands, the skin roughened by work in a peasant home, holding Jesus. I thought of Joseph's hands, the hands of a carpenter, skin thickened by his trade, teaching Jesus to walk. Rough but caring hands, comforting, clothing, feeding the baby. Hard hands, but softened by love.

As the baby grew, the hand of God was rough in Jesus' life. From wilderness experience to the life of a wandering teacher, it wasn't easy being God's son. He had to face the doubt, the questions, the growing hatred, and the rejection of the establishment. And, finally, the cross. And there the soldiers' hands were rough, calloused and callous, and so was the wood. No softness there.

But through the roughness, love was let loose into the world. A love alternately gentle and abrasive, comforting and challenging, pruning and healing.

And because of the roughness, the suffering and the pain in Jesus' life, the poor of Nicaragua can recognize God-with-us and identify with him. If the hand of God had been only gentle he would have been less relevant, easier to ignore.

Lord, it's so easy
to sentimentalize your story.
To let the drifts of Christmas snow,
so clean, pollution free,
cover the rough edges of real life.
So tempting to recreate you
in an image more to my taste.
To crystallize the fruit of suffering
into something sweeter,
and clothe reality in silk
rather than sackcloth.
Rewrite your gospel,
and make your coming —
and your going, Lord —
a charming tale
acceptable in all the best circles.
The suffering and the violence removed,
a home video suitable for all the family.

The truth is different,
and it must be so
if it's to be relevant to life.
No yuppie, you, Lord.
No census average,
the awkward corners smoothed away,
your lifestyle simplified
to fit the market research.
The junk mail bouncing through your letter box.
You were a carpenter
who knew the unplaned edge of things,
and felt the splinters of rejection.
Took rough with smooth —
more rough than smooth, I think —
and welcomed suffering,
not for its own sake,
but to identify yourself
with those who suffer.
The rough handed poor
who scrape their knuckles
in the stony soil of want.

At times, forgive me, Lord,
in arrogance,
I think I have a God to share with them,
something to teach.

But then I realize
you're nearer them than me.
And learning has to be the other way.
Their God, rough handed,
sometimes hungry,
without a place to put his head,
is calling me to face reality.

That's hard to take.
May I just think about it, Lord?

"Working on the Hedge"

John 12:1-3

I WAS leading a church conference recently. We were looking at the story of Mary pouring the perfume over Jesus' feet, and thinking about the reactions of the people involved. They were real human beings, not cardboard cutouts, and we tried to imagine how they felt. Martha was busy with the cooking. We thought of the smell of food, the buzz of conversation. We saw the disciples relaxing at the end of the day, mixing with other guests who were curious about this new teacher. We pictured Jesus himself, looking around, reading people's attitudes, gauging their needs.

We tried to grasp some of the feelings floating around the room. Feelings of friendship, anticipation, warmth. Then someone surprised us. "What about the apprehension?" he asked, "What about the fear?"

It started a new train of thought. Perhaps it wasn't such a comfortable experience being around Jesus then. Just a short time before, he'd raised Lazarus from the dead — Mary and Martha's brother. Lazarus himself was with them at the meal. Ordinary people didn't have that sort of power, didn't do things like that. Who was this Jesus, and what was he going to do next?

And remembering what he'd done, so recently, for Mary's family, helps us towards understanding Mary's extravagant gesture with the perfume. Washing the feet of a guest is still part of some Eastern cultures today. Mary was simply taking this custom and enlarging it, adding to its significance. She was responding to what had happened, to what Jesus had done. It was an intuitive action, a gift straight from the heart, rather than from the mind. And none the worse for that. For the onlookers it was another startling event to think about.

Jesus' presence _can_ bring comfort, but it can also disturb. It's a loving presence, but it's also a powerful one that demands a response. We can't meet Jesus and be the same afterwards. We may think we're sitting down to a quiet meal with him, but it's quite likely to turn into an event that shakes all our assumptions, changes our world. Jesus can be disturbing to know.

Lord, sometimes, my only defence against you
is to pick out the comfortable bits
of your story,
and cling to them.
Hold on to the warmth, the friendship,
the meals with friends,
the many kindnesses and acts of healing,
and pretend that's all there is.

I can accept a comfortable Christ,
who wipes my tears away,
and holds my hands
and leads me in green pastures.
It's pleasant country, that.
Perpetual holiday.

But it's a self-deluding game.
A blind man's bluff
in which I tie the blindfold on myself,
and never try to reach out for the truth,
content with twilight.

Yet, underneath the gentle Jesus bit,
I sense your strength.
A power, reaching to the heart of things.
A knowledge that penetrates pretence,
cuts through the roles I play,
removes the masks.
Sees me as I am, and shows me to myself.
It's not a pretty sight, I know,
that's why I spend my time
trying to cover it up.
To hide, not just from you, but from myself.

But you are my reality.
To sit with you is like no other meal.
The bread and wine no ordinary fare.
Your presence hurts in honesty,
disturbs,
and strips defences bare.
But then in tenderness,
before I can despair,
you offer to rebuild, renew,
and love takes on a new responsibility.
Building, from the bones of my dissection,
a new creation.

25

Ephesians 2:13-18

TWO pictures come to my mind from the Berlin Wall. The first is of a young man with a small hammer, enthusiastically chipping away at the concrete. He didn't seem to be getting very far. His hammer just bounced off the great blocks. People around him were cheering, but I felt he'd finish up with a headache and a sore arm.

The second picture was of men driving earthmoving equipment at the wall. With their diggers and cranes, they dislodged great graffiti-covered chunks of it to more cheers.

I remember a visit to both sides of Berlin a few years ago. After meeting Christian friends in the East, we stood quietly on the Western side of the wall and looked at three crosses. There were many more, scattered along its length, each marking the death by shooting of someone who'd tried unsuccessfully to get to freedom. "Unbekannt", it said on the crosses, "Unknown".

Why do we put up walls? We surround our lives with them, walls of suspicion and fear. Walls of unfriendliness. We're very careful who we allow into our own space. We all have our personal checkpoints at which people have to prove themselves to be harmless, to think like we do, to conform, before we let them in.

We think the walls are for our own protection, but really they hem us in, limit our freedom. The East German authorities said the Berlin Wall was to protect their people from the West. In reality it stopped them leaving.

Jesus came to bring us full life (John 10:10). We enter it by knocking down our personal walls and opening doors, not by installing mental locks and bars and passport checks. Sometimes, God's content to watch us chip away at our own walls slowly with a little hammer, but there are times when he seems to prefer the bulldozer.

Lord, I need your help today,
in breaking out.
The walls I've made,
and thought were good and comforting,
now threaten me.
I've shut my gate on life secure,
and bolted it.
All to protect my shopsoiled wisdom,
bargain priced and cheaply bought.
Plastic pearls, not worth the keeping.

But when I think about it, Lord,
it's not security I've found, but prison.
I'm self-confined within the walls I've built,
my fear of change the jailor.
I sit, reluctant,
trying to retain my grasp
on the false security
of life lived timidly.

And when with new found courage
I start to chip away the wall,
my hammer bounces off, with small effect,
my little efforts useless.

Give me your strength, Lord,
to face the world afresh.
To make a move that takes me
from the sterile shelter of my fears
into your light outside.
That's where real life begins.
And grows.

It's late, Lord.
I've lived so long inside the walls.
But in my new gained freedom,
the casualties of my fears,
strewn round the perimeter of my defences,
stir into life.

Joy and adventure,
long alien to me,
reach out and welcome.
I feel the sunshine,
hear the birdsong of renewal.
See your face again.

Romans 8:26-27

EDDIE Neale is an Anglican minister whose Nottingham parish was a housing estate with many problems. I suppose it's more accurate to say it was the people who had the problems, and caused many of them, although the environment in which they lived didn't help much.

He describes his work in a very moving book *Rivers in a Dry Land*. He writes of his experiences in counselling people needing help.

"I'm paid to 'help' people," he writes, "but I'm wary of people who try to fix their problem on me . . . I dodge. Even if I could fix it . . . I don't think that's the best help I can offer."

It's so easy to project our trouble onto someone else. Off-load it, act helpless, and hope he'll deal with it for us. And if we're not told what to do in three easy lessons then we can blame him instead of ourselves if the problem's not solved.

Eddie Neale's point is that it's not usually realistic to hope for fairy-tale solutions. It's better for all, particularly the one with the problem, if he's helped to solve it for himself. That's how we discover our own strengths. And if we can't solve it, then we have to learn to rely on God, and live within the situation, even though we don't understand why.

It's a picture, too, of the way we sometimes try to use God. Certainly God wants us to go to him with our problems, to talk them through with him, but my experience strongly suggests that we shouldn't expect a magic wand reply. The hard fact is that loving though God is, he doesn't always come up with a neat solution, doesn't always tie up the loose ends in my life. Life can be painful, even for believers. Miracles do happen, but not all the time. That's why we call them miracles.

What God does in these situations is to surround us with his love, and support us while we find the strength to face what's troubling us. His spirit agonizes with us, helps us find our own way. And if a solution is beyond our grasp, if it's something we have to live with, then you can be sure he'll be there, living through it with us.

That's all part of his love, nurturing us into growth.

Lord, when life's hard, and puzzling,
and I can't see the way ahead,
it would be so much easier
if you did everything for me.
Answered my questions.
Dealt with my problems.
Bulldozed a road
right through the wilderness,
and signposted it, just so.
Life could be so much smoother
if you helped a little more.

A coin in the slot God,
who let me win
each time I pulled the handle.
I'd like that, Lord.
No worry, never any risk.
I could relax,
and concentrate on loving you.

Cupboard love, I hear you say?
Well, yes, you have a point.
If loving you depended on the way
you fixed the path,
it wouldn't have much value.
The lowest form of payment.
Tit for tat.

And would I want it round the other way?
That your love too
depended on my doing everything just so?
I'd be in quite a hole if that were true.
If love were measured out by what I'd earned,
there wouldn't be so much of it about.

But, thank you Lord,
it doesn't work like that.
Your love's available for free,
and loving wisdom says
the struggle that I face
is part and parcel of your love.
My problems come, not in spite of love,
but because of it.
You gather up the pains into your plan,
and draw me to yourself,
mature and stronger than I was before.

John 3:3-8

I WAS surprised to discover that the first recorded composer of European music was a twelfth century nun. Recorded in a manuscript, I hasten to add, not on a cassette! She described herself, poetically, as "a feather on the breath of God".

Maybe she meant that musically, God being her inspiration. I don't know, but it's a lovely image.

Something, someone, utterly at God's command. Ready for the Spirit's direction. Sensitive, trembling at the least movement. Surrendered to his will. Carried along by his strength.

Not only does the breath of God give a sense of purpose, but it gives life itself. We're told that when God made humanity he "breathed into his nostrils the breath of life . . ." (Genesis 2:7).

But the image breaks down if it's carried too far. We're not lightweight creatures, weakly giving in to every wind that blows. We're not completely inanimate feathers, totally helpless on God's breath. As human beings, created in God's image, we may ". . . live and move and have our being in him . . ." (Acts 17:28), but we can usually choose the direction we'll go and the response we make.

That's the joy of Christian life, and also its responsibility.

Lord, sitting silently
I hear the stirring of the wind.
Invisible, gentle.
Fluttering the curtains
at the windows of my life.
Lifting an edge
and letting in the air.
Shuffling the papers of my faith
to rearrange them
more to your liking.

The breeze feels good.
It cools and soothes,
and reassures me.
Takes command,
and indicates
both route and destination
of my pilgrimage.

But sometimes, Lord,
the wind blows harder.
Ruffles my hair.
Shakes out the cobwebs of content
that clutter up the corners of my room.
Reminds me of my own responsibilities.
My need to choose,
decide direction, purpose.

I am no feather,
blown by every wind,
but your creation,
body, soul and will.
Mind, Lord, and will.
Given me for use, not decoration.
Fresh fashioned
for your spirit's dwelling place.
Not as a monument,
fast rooted in the earth,
static,
but vital,
part of your dynamic purpose,
which is love.

Acts 7:48-53

I WOKE up one morning with a stiff neck. It was very painful. Fortunately, Jenny, my physiotherapist daughter, was staying with us at the time.

She probed and pressed, and located a joint that was locked and causing the pain. She began to manipulate my neck. At first, it was just a gentle turning, this way and that. Then she began to pull and twist more strongly.

Now, I've a lot of confidence in her. On other occasions she'd treated a back pain successfully, but the pressure and strength she was using suddenly scared me.

I tried to relax, but couldn't. I felt all my muscles tensing up, resisting what she was trying to do. I knew, intellectually, that she could help but I still fought her. She had to give up, temporarily. Instead, she put a bag of frozen peas on my neck, to encourage circulation and to dull the ache before she tried again.

This time her treatment worked, and I was halfway to being human again, a little miracle in itself.

We often fight the love God offers. We treat him as an intruder. Fight against his hands in our lives as though he were trying to injure, rather than heal. Sometimes his presence does bring pain, particularly when we start to face the need to change and grow. But even the pain can be used constructively, for good.

"Relax," said Jenny, and, hard though it was to do it, I saw the point. If only we would relax in God, accept his presence as the blessing it is, he'd be able to help us more.

Jenny's parting advice was that I should do some simple regular exercises to keep my neck muscles working. There's another point there, but I won't labour it.

Lord, you don't have an easy time
dealing with me.
I use the right words,
wear all the appropriate labels,
and profess to trust you,
but when the moment comes
to put myself completely in your hands,
my lifestyle says I don't.
My words and deeds
don't seem to synchronize,
their contradictory signals just confuse.

I come to you for help,
but when it's offered
I'm not sure I want it, after all.
I'd rather choose an easier way.
Your presence sometimes
seems to threaten, Lord, rather than heal,
and your requests can work out hard.

And what I'm struggling to say,
although the words are hard to find,
is that I don't have an easy time, either,
dealing with you.

You tell me to relax,
and put my trust in you,
to let you take the strain.
But that's not easy, Lord,
for one who's always tried
to organize himself, manage his time,
and stay on top of things.
There's still a bit of me,
a lot of me, to tell the truth,
that wants to do it my own way.
You know the song.

Lord, all I can do
is ask, once more, for help.
Not just to solve immediate problems
but to help let them go.
To find the grace
to put my life and being
firmly in your care.
Open my hands, loosen my grip,
and wait for you.

Matthew 5:11-15

A SEVERE blizzard blanketed large parts of England with unexpected snow. It brought down power lines, and many homes were without electricity for several days. In one stroke people were reminded forcefully of what life was like for everyone in times past. Only open fires to cook with, only candles and small oil lamps for light.

It was like that in Jesus' time. I own a small oil lamp from Roman times, found in Palestine. It's moulded in red clay, and consists simply of a small reservoir for oil, and a little hole for a simple cotton wick. The light it gave was meagre and dim. At best, it illuminated only a small area of a room. Even in the homes of the wealthy, who could afford a cluster of candles or a hanging lamp with several wicks, the light was feeble.

So when Jesus spoke to the people in the Jerusalem temple, he was using a vivid metaphor, something to catch the attention. "I am the light of the world," he said, "Whoever follows me will never walk in darkness, but will have the light of life" (John 8:12).

Imagine, in a culture of candles and oil lamps, a light so great that darkness is driven away. Only the sun could do that, but here was a man claiming the same. Claiming more in fact, because the sun doesn't shine at night.

Jesus was claiming that his words and life revealed the truth about God in a way never done before. That in him, through him, light would shine, chasing away the fear and ignorance that darken life.

But in Matthew's gospel, Jesus tells his disciples that they are the light of the world. So which is it? Is he the light, or are they?

In the Russian Orthodox Church, at Easter, the priest brings a lighted candle. Worshippers each light their own candle from his, or from a neighbour's, the light increasing as more flames are lit. Taking light from the source, passed on one to another, it's the same light, yet different, because each candle is different. And as the light passes, the dim glow brightens, and the whole church is illuminated.

We take our light from his, and we are called to stand against the dark. But shedding light isn't without cost. Someone said, although I don't remember who, "If you want to be a candle you have to suffer the burning."

Candle flame of life

Lord, there are times
when I'm tempted to give up.
When all the pressures of my world,
darken my vision,
wear down my will.
And, footweary and head low,
I find it all a burden hard to bear.
Standing against the powers of the age
seems futile.
Don Quixote without a donkey.

My world looks dark,
my faith a dusty relic
seen dimly through the smeared glass
of a museum showcase,
long unvisited.
The fossil bones of faith dust covered.
A prehistoric curiosity.
Hard to believe those bones
were once the stuff of life.

And yet, within the dark,
the candles glow.
Frail flames of flickering light.
Will-o'-the-wisps of faith,
now here, now there,
but leading to fulfilment.
As one seems quenched
another glows,
sparks into light.
Darkness is distanced,
and, in light's small flame,
hope warms its hands.

And I am strengthened to renew my trust
in love, alive and well.
In time,
in God's own time,
the flames will grow
and coalesce into a dawn
when earth is filled with light
from end to end.

Meanwhile, Lord, I'll gather up my courage
for one more day.

Knowing that weak though I am —
and foolish Lord, but let's not dwell on that —
you are at work,
blowing the ashes of my life into new flame.

"In the Deep Midwinter"

A. D. ASKEW

John 1:1-5

DURING the Gulf War, a column of British armoured cars was attacked by United States aircraft. It was a tragic error, and nine British soldiers died. One was a young man, uninjured in the initial attack, who went back into the blazing vehicle three times to try to rescue comrades. Making the third attempt, he was killed by ammunition exploding in the flames.

Sadly, we can all recognize the presence of evil in the world. The evil that creates dictators, the evil that makes people kill for power. We recognize accident too. The tragic circumstances of quick action made under pressure, resulting in suffering and death. Sometimes, often, it seems that that's how the world works — on evil or, at best, accident.

But then something else enters the story. A young man, in the middle of gut-wrenching danger when instinct shouts "Run! Get out of it!", actually stops and then goes back to save his friends.

He dies, but he leaves behind more than a hint of goodness. Caught up in the horror of war, he tries to help others, as many have before him. He didn't succeed, but he tried. And this goodness lights up the darkness in which we seem to be living.

It tells us that there's something else besides evil and accident at the centre of existence. He'd probably hoot with embarrassed laughter if he could read these words, but what he showed so vividly was love. The urge to help, the concern for others that puts itself at risk.

So often, evil looms large, seems all powerful. But somehow it never quite overwhelms the good. The light shines on, and there is still hope. Darkness never quite overcomes it.

When people ask me how I can believe in face of so much evil, all I can say is how can I not, in face of so much good? As Louis McNiece, the poet, once said, "There will be sunlight later, and the equation will come out in the end."

Lord of all goodness,
there are moments, I confess,
when doubt rules strong.
Moments of darkness
when life seems bleak,
your promises little short of mockery.
The wind rips through my life,
stripping the leaves,
straining the roots,
threatening to tear me
from my hold on you.
It whips the questions from my lips
before I find the breath to ask them.

Lord, my mind can't cope.
It's hard to see a pattern in the dark.
Harder still to see an underlying purpose,
when suffering throws its shadow,
and hope's eclipsed.
Christian clichés bring no comfort.
The candle flame of faith
gives little light.

And yet, Lord, still it burns,
the candle flame.
Live and persistent.
It may not seem a lot,
no floodlight glare,
no firework flash of coloured light,
but, somehow,
nothing seems to put it out.
Not quite.
It dims, dark edged with doubt,
struggles, then suddenly,
the very wind that threatened its existence
fans it to life.
The flame burns brighter,
and its glow sets light to other candles
I'd not thought were there.

And as the darkness distances
I see, beyond the shadow of the cross,
the dawning light of resurrection.
Darkness is strong, but you are stronger.
I leave the pattern and the purpose
in your hands.

Mark 7:14-23

THE American experience of the Vietnam war has produced a number of cinema films. The worst have created cardboard heroes, glorifying *machismo* and violence. The best have tried to examine the roots of violence within the soldiers themselves.

"Platoon" followed a group of young American infantrymen through the horrors of combat. It looked at the fear which spawned the violence. It made no excuses, and it was honest enough to acknowledge that terror and atrocity were not limited to one side of the struggle. There were no knights in shining armour.

Towards the end of the film, a young soldier says, "We didn't fight the enemy. We fought ourselves. The enemy was within."

That's where he always is. The enemy's the fear that rises so easily from the depths of our being when we feel threatened. It may be an over-simplification, but when you look at how wars begin, the aggressor usually starts by convincing his own people that they're in danger themselves. That's the fear that sows the seeds of anger which grow into violence.

For most of us, automatic rifles are out of reach, and the anger doesn't turn to killing. Not other people anyway. But it can be murder on ourselves. The anger, endlessly replaying old tapes of wrongs, real or imaginary, sours our lives. Breeds mistrust, cynicism, hardness.

The answer? That's the hard one. Perhaps acknowledging that the enemy is within, trying to recognize the way we project our anger onto others, and understanding that we're often saddling other people with our own fear.

Lord, the anger's there
however much I may deny it.
I use the Christian clichés,
speak of love and service,
walking second miles.
But still it's there.

Resentment, irritation,
when things don't go my way.
The bitter comment,
smokescreened with a smile,
disguised as disappointment.

But underneath I'm seething.
Flexing claws and twitching tail,
I wait to pounce and scratch and bite.
Forgiveness stored away
in some locked cupboard of my mind.
Unopened, and the key misplaced.

Lord, won't you force the door?
Break in, throw out the rubbish long accumulated,
dust down the love locked in
and give it space to grow?
Begin to turn the battlefield into a garden?

But even as I ask,
I know the answer lies with me.
It lies with me to make a move,
to recognize just where I'm at,
and why.
And then to work with you
towards that partnership of love,
not forced, but freely given,
that casts out fear.

Lord, help me struggle free
from all that holds me back,
and start me on the road
towards shalom.

Mark 4:35-41

I WAS on the beach, sketching. I was absorbed, working out the structure of the painting, the light passages, the darks, mixing the colours. All was sunshine and warmth.

Suddenly, I felt a cold breeze on my back. A deep shadow raced over where I was sitting. I looked behind and saw a great black cloud filling the sky. The sun had disappeared, and within a couple of minutes I was heading for the cover of the car, trying to protect the wet watercolour from the heavy splashes of rain, the first of the storm.

With fishermen among them, perhaps the disciples in the boat were more aware of the weather and its sudden changes. But this storm scared them.

They woke Jesus, who was asleep on a cushion. I like that little bit of authentic, almost inconsequential, detail — a cushion. The bare wooden seats of a fishing boat can be very hard. Did Jesus' back ache sometimes, after a busy day, like mine does?

"Don't you care?" they ask. There's another question wrapped up in that one. "And can't you do anything about it?"

Jesus saw their fear, their need. He put out his arm, and the storm was stilled. The disciples were amazed, awestruck, by the miracle. But it seems to me that the most far reaching miracle in life isn't when Jesus does what we ask him to do, but when we do what he asks us to do.

Perhaps even he's a little bit surprised when we actually obey him.

The summer waves break gently, Lord.
Sun glistens gold into my eyes.
Water and sand run warmly through my toes.
Air, salt on tongue.
Sea chattering the shingle, soft through stones.

It's all so warm and comfortable, Lord.
The way I like my faith to be.
A picnic on the beach.
Nothing to challenge or demand.
And towel-wrapped in the familiar,
I can doze away my days
sheltered behind the windbreak of pious platitudes,
never questioned.

But life with you is more than this.
You call me, Lord, to deeper waters.
To cast off and sail
from the polluted outfalls of the shore.

It scares me, Lord.
I'm frightened by the sea,
its depth and width,
its unseen currents, changing moods, uncertainties.
It runs to storm,
to waves and gale-force winds.
And out of sight of land
I feel so vulnerable and alone.

Yet that's not so.
Amid the storm
I sense your presence, power.
Your arm stretched out.
Your voice above the wind.
The reassuring words
"Peace, be still."

And in the wind-drop quiet,
the storm within me
is the storm you still.
The peace you bring
not only to the wind,
but to my restless spirit.
A transformation triggered by your love.
Fear falls away,
a little at a time —

have patience with me, Lord —
and I am ready to sail on.
Through calm or squall,
or sudden beauty.

Not searching for safe harbour,
or land across the sea,
but carrying love's cargo,
the riches of your presence.
And in its new-world gold of revelation
I begin to see with joyful clarity,
and greater wonder still,
I do not journey to,
but with.

You are the sea,
the storm,
the stillness,
and the ship.

"On the Patio"

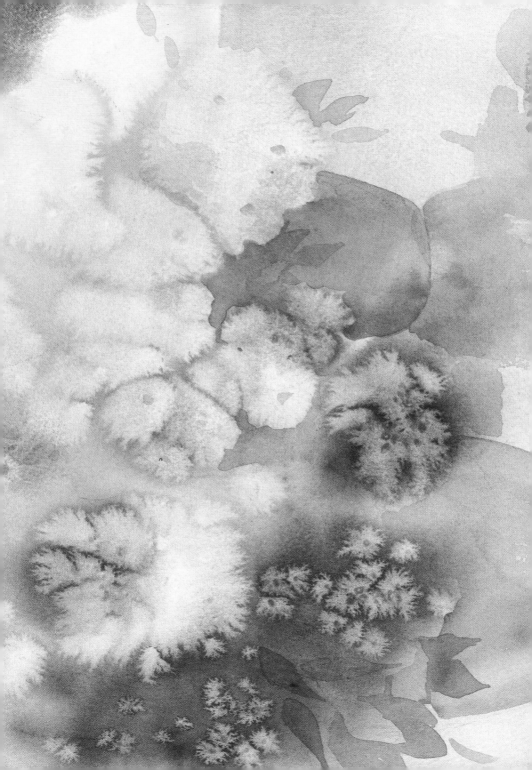

Matthew 25:34-40

WALKING around Peterborough Cathedral, I saw the notice-board covered with slips of paper. Each was a request for prayer. Some asked for prayers for soldiers and airmen in the Persian Gulf. Others spoke of family problems. Some were signed, some were anonymous.

One in particular moved me. It was written by a teenage girl. It said:

"Please pray for my friend. She's fourteen years old and is H.I.V. positive. Most people don't want to know her any more, but she needs my love."

I'm sure both of them needed love, and still do.

When AIDS was first recognized, people looked for causes. Not just the virus, but for why it was happening. It was easy, then, to pick out particular lifestyles, and blame sufferers for creating their own problems by the way they lived. That's not so easy any more, and wasn't a very compassionate way of looking at it anyway.

It seems to me that with any sort of suffering we should look beyond the causes and reasons, beyond the "blame", and ask what love can do to help.

A new problem always creates fear at the beginning, and we all feel the need to find something, someone, to hold responsible. But we need to get behind that to the heart of the suffering. Each generation has to learn its own compassion, find its own response to people in crisis.

The challenge to me lies in the familiar words in Matthew 25. Whether it's the hungry and thirsty, the naked or sick, or those in prison, Jesus doesn't talk about blame. He simply asks whether we helped or not.

Presumably most people in prison could be said to have done something to have got themselves there, although that's probably too simplistic an approach, both in Jesus' day and our own. However we look at it, it doesn't seem to be the main point for him. Jesus asks, "Did you love them? Did you do anything to help?"

That unknown teenager in Peterborough can teach me a thing or two.

Lord, she said it all,
the girl in Peterborough.
While I look for a scapegoat
when things go wrong,
she tries to love.

It's all so easy, Lord,
to take a stance in righteous indignation.
To claim some sort of moral vantage point
from which to view the depths below.
Throw out my condemnation from the bench
where I'm both judge and jury,
and prosecution too.
Find someone, anyone,
on whom to heap the blame,
and turn away, untouched.
"Their own fault, after all . . .",
as though that wrapped it up
and I could keep my conscience clean.

The trouble is
the vantage point of cold morality's a lonely place.
I stand there on a pedestal of my own making.
No room for anyone but me, and you.

But when I look around, I find you've gone.
Your place is empty.
And suddenly I see you, standing down below
with those I thought condemned.
My pedestal too cold a place for you.

And then you look at me
and smile, and say,
"No need to feel alone,
come down and join me where I am,
with these who need my love."

Your love's not carved in stone,
a marble angel on a graveyard plinth.
It stirs the blood,
gives life and hope,
eases the pain of daily living.

Lord, take me back to innocence,
where love is love
and blame's beside the point.

Luke 22:19-20

LEONARDO da Vinci's painting of "The Last Supper" is well known. It's a mural — painted directly onto a wall. The twelve disciples are all grouped around Jesus on the far side of the table and down to the ends.

The near side, nearest the spectator, is empty.

It's a convention that's used a lot on stage and in films. The side of any table nearest the viewer is left empty, so that nothing is obscured. You can see the faces of everyone involved in the drama. There are no shoulders to look over.

I believe there's another reason too. The viewer takes his place at the table, not just as a spectator, but as a participant. We share in the drama, there's a place at the table for us. That's what makes it real.

So, too, with the painting. A great work of art, truly, but rather more. It was painted on the end wall of a refectory — the dining room — of a monastery. When the monks sat down to eat, their tables were a continuation of the table on the wall. They were dining with Jesus. Every meal was with him.

"This is my body, broken for you," said Jesus. Not just for the original twelve gathered around, but for all of us willing to take our place at the table.

We share in the reality, not simply gaze at an interpretation. The host at the table invites us to join him, asks for our involvement.

Lord, I hardly dare accept
the invitation.
I want to sit with you,
to hear your words,
to share the meal.
To stretch across the table,
take the bread and wine
straight from your hands.
I want to join the others
grouped around you.

But something makes me hesitate,
hold back,
and wonder at the worth you place on me.
That you, God's son,
whatever that may really mean,
the mystery's too deep for me,
should hold an open house
for ordinary folk.

Offering your body,
coarse ground
between the millstones of rejection.
Your blood, trod out
beneath shod feet
which trample, unconcerned,
on holiness.

I'd settle for much less, Lord,
some slight acknowledgement,
in passing,
that you care,
but not the lengths to which you go
to show your love.

And yet why should I be content
to live on crumbs
from underneath the table,
when I can see
your love's already set a place
across the board,
and put my name on it.

And as I start to realize
the riches that you offer,
I daren't do other than accept.

And as I take my seat,
wondering just what to say or do,
I understand
I'm not a transitory guest,
my welcome soon outlived,
but one of the family.
My place secure,
my presence welcomed.

"Sunshine After Rain"

1 John 4:7-11

I'M a collector. I love and respect old things. Antiques, old paintings, antiquarian books. From time to time, I get lists of old books for sale, sent to me by antiquarian booksellers. The format is always the same. Each book is listed by author, then comes the title, the date of the particular edition, and then anything else that's relevant. The size, the style of binding, and so on.

Booksellers have their own jargon of course, and all this is written in abbreviation. Quite often, at the end of a short description of a particular book, you'll see the letters WAF. They stand for "with all faults". When you see this, you know that the dealer is warning you that the book is imperfect. It has faults. Perhaps some pages are missing, or it's suffered significant damage. He's found some faults but he thinks there may be more. If you really want the book, you have to accept it as it is.

I like to think that's the way God loves us. With all faults. And that, in spite of our faults, he's still prepared to accept us as we are, "buy" us, redeem us, and add us to his collection. God doesn't demand perfection before he loves us. He loves us as we are, with all faults.

Someone said, "There is nothing that we can say or do to make God love us more than he already does."

That's important. He accepts us as we are. Having accepted us, he then begins to work with us, renewing, repairing, recreating us and our lives, but that's nothing to do with how he loves us. And, when you think about it, it has to be that way, because if God loved us more the better we became, it would imply that God loves some people more and other people less. And that can't be true.

It would also mean that we could earn God's love and, again, that's not on. Love is his free gift, and he gives it to us as we are, with all our faults.

If that's the way God loves us, then maybe that's the way we ought to love each other.

Lord, the promise of your love
makes me uncomfortable.
Somehow, I'd rather earn it,
than take it as a gift.
Pretend that, through my own hard work,
I've done something to deserve it.

To think that you should love me as I am,
with all faults, no strings attached,
doesn't seem quite right.
I'd rather pile up Brownie points,
work my way towards the goal,
and feel I've been successful,
won the prize.

But when I look inside myself,
dig down a bit,
I find it's pride that's talking.
A pride that doesn't want to take
your gift of love,
or any other gift, for free.
Rather stand on my own two feet,
self-made.

And then I realize
that even when I feel like this,
inclined to turn my back, go my own way,
your love's still there.

Over me and under me.
Before me and behind me.
Around me and within me.

Your love encompassing.

The generosity is overwhelming.
I find it hard to understand —
I'm still wriggling, Lord —
hard to understand
why you should offer it at all.
Until I realize
it isn't just an act of love
that takes me as I am.
Love is your nature.
You are love, and love can do no other.
Love can only love.

And when I look afresh
at who I am, and how I live,
I feel the secret's
not to try to understand
the mystery of love
but simply to relax in it.
Relax in you,
and let the tide of love
flow in with joy.

The joy of knowing
that, with all my faults,
you treasure me.

"January Frost"

Isaiah 53:1-3

THE church I attend is close to an estate of five high-rise residential blocks of apartments. Some of the blocks are fourteen storeys high, great concrete towers, stark, square, unlovely, dwarfing the church building. Even the church spire only reaches to about the sixth floor level of the nearest block.

When most of Europe's parish churches were built, centuries ago, they dominated everything else. They were much taller than the single storey cottages of the poor, higher than the two or three storey houses of the merchants. The cathedrals rivalled the castles of the barons. Strong stone walls, high towers, all spoke of a church of power, assertive, self-confident.

Today's buildings mirror a different reality. In a society of openly material values, the secular overshadows the church. And the church's role has become what perhaps it always should have been, a struggling, even suffering, community. Identifying more with the poor than the powerful, although let's not forget that the powerful need God as much as the poor do.

Power for the church lies not in its wealth and great buildings, but in its loving service. And its service must be out there in the loneliness so often found in the tower blocks, rather than offered from the warm security of the church.

Lord, it's hard to comprehend,
harder to accept.
It goes against the grain,
and I don't like the idea
one little bit.
The suffering.
The self-denial.
I'd rather sing "Onward Christian soldiers"
and believe myself part of a mighty army
sweeping everything before it.
Exploding my nuclear warheads
of devastating truth,
vaporizing opposition,
the only mark they leave
a shadow on the wall.
All powerful, and in control.

My grouse, if I'm permitted one,
is that you give me no encouragement.
Whenever I'm belligerent,
and try to put the opposition down —
in your name, Lord, it's all for you,
that's what I tell myself —
you hold me back.
Or so it seems.
Your voice comes quietly,
insistently,
annoyingly at times,
reminding me that's not your way.

If you would bring your kingdom in by power
you'd probably not need my help.
But living wisdom says —
and that's another name for you —
that power can force a hand to work,
but not a heart to love.
Your methods seem a little weak,
and up for question, Lord,
by this world's standards.
But love's survived so far,
and it's the only thing I know
that grows and thrives by giving.

Philippians 4:4-9

A CONCERT in Rome brought together three of the loveliest tenor voices in the world of opera. José Carreras, Luciano Pavarotti, and Placido Domingo. There was some superb singing, and much comment. Carreras, they said, had a voice of silver. Pavarotti, an unmatched dramatic quality. Domingo, a richness of sound seldom heard.

Someone asked, "But who's the best?" It seemed a superficial and unnecessary question. One better not answered, because there is no answer. How do you judge? They were all superb, each bringing unique, personal qualities into his music.

Is an apple better than an orange or a mango? You may like one more than another, but none is "best". It's a false question.

I wonder why we so often bring this element of competition into life. Why do we think that dominance is so important? Does it matter who's "best"? And will it make the singer's voice any better than it is already? Let's simply accept the beauty of the voice, the individual interpretation of the music, and rejoice in it.

There's no competitive edge in the Christian faith, the strongest is weak, the precedence is turned upside down. I notice that when St. Paul refers to true and noble things, lovely things, he asks us to "fill all your thoughts with them," as another translation puts it. It's an attitude that adds to our quality of life in a way that competitiveness never can. There's no top ten in righteousness. We share in his kingdom, not by being better than anyone else, but because he loves us. And he does that equally, whoever we are.

I love the words, Lord,
joy, gentleness and peace.
I'd give my vote for them at any time.
They're all I want,
at least, in quiet moments,
when I'm all alone with you.
To stay here, world forgotten,
mind's doors and windows
double locked against intruders.

Just you and me.
And in the quiet, Lord,
it's not too difficult
to fill my mind with thoughts
of all that's good and beautiful.

At least, that's what I try to tell myself.
But when I face the truth —
and truth's a nuisance
I could sometimes do without —
I have to admit
to just a touch of self-deception.
It's what I'd like to happen, Lord,
but even here, just you and me,
I can't hold on to it for long.
My mind's a nomad,
packing up and moving on
without a moment's notice.
And all the joy and beauty,
peace and truth,
get left behind,
like campfire ashes, quickly cold.

Lord, when I face the world again,
with all its tensions, fears, and sinfulness,
I'd like to carry with me
some shadow of the beauty
that I find in you.
Some echo of the mystery of your love.
A point of reference,
that helps me recognize
the true and good,
whenever and wherever met,
and helps me share some semblance of your peace
with other travellers along the road.

Hebrews 12:1-3

ABOUT fifty of us met to celebrate a special occasion with a Christian minister. We'd all been members of a church he'd led, years ago. It was the fifty-first anniversary of the beginning of his time there. After twenty or more years he'd moved on, but many of us had kept in touch. Some had stayed at the church the whole time, others hadn't.

He was eighty-five. Still lively in mind and faith, and straight in body, although maybe just a little bit stiff. His sense of humour was still intact, and he was still preaching regularly.

The afternoon was warm with sun, memory and matured friendship. The air was full of "Do you remember . . .?" Creased, dog-eared black and white photographs had been resurrected for the day. They showed young, uncreased faces smiling out of yesterday's fashions.

Each person had been profoundly influenced by this one man. Each life had gone its own course. Some had been very successful in this world's terms, others not so. Many treasured happy relationships, a few were tinged with sadness, even tragedy.

I wondered how he felt, seeing us all together. Did he feel successful, or what? It seemed an intrusion to ask. And the more I thought about the question, the less it seemed to matter.

What did matter was his life. He'd lived it faithfully, consistently. He'd preached his vision of the truth, and lived it out as honestly as he could. At times he'd been misunderstood. He'd had his share of criticism, but he'd always accepted it graciously, and he'd stayed true. His influence, the values he'd lived out, could be seen in the people around him that afternoon.

The results? The success? Not for us to judge, but it looked pretty good from where I was sitting. And I thanked God for him.

Lord, at times
it's hard to identify
with patriarchs of long ago.
I know the stories well,
but they are heroes grown large
across the centuries,
striding in seven league boots
across a distant landscape,
their relevance not obvious to me.
My twentieth century sophistication
unready for their certainties.

The cloud of witnesses feels far away.
Insubstantial.
My life seems wreathed in mist at times,
and I can't see the way.
Faith's fogged and shadowy.

But when I concentrate on now,
and see the faith proclaimed
in living flesh and blood,
not just in words but life,
the focus sharpens.
Becomes believable.
Seeing an individual journey charted,
laid out in lives around him,
his navigation straight on course
in spite of rocks and other hazards on his way,
tells me it's possible.
Possible both to believe
and stay faithful.

Lord, I'm no hallmarked hero,
more your genuine twenty-two carat coward.
So easily discouraged.
The least thing said or done,
the smallest criticism, the slightest obstacle,
and I'm all for surrender.

The trouble is
the things that matter, don't,
the things that don't, do,
if you get my meaning.
My values are so easily disturbed,
the pattern overturned,
constantly changing and re-forming,
like a mad kaleidoscope.

Lord, in the pressures of today,
help me to understand
that all your witnesses were human,
just like me.
And prone to questioning and fear and doubt,
as I am.
And yet each one a sharer
in the strength which you hold out
to all who trust and try.

I'm not sure, Lord, if that makes living easier,
but it makes it possible,
at least for today.
And that's where I begin.

"Wind From the Sea, Norfolk"

Luke 18:9-14

A DOCTOR friend of mine told me about a patient who phoned early one morning. "Please can I come to see you? It's urgent." My friend's appointment list was full, but he told the man to come anyway, promising to fit him in as soon as he could. The man came and sat in the waiting room.

After some time, the doctor called for him. "Sorry," said the receptionist, "he's gone. He said he couldn't wait any longer or he'd miss his prayer time. He said he'd come back later."

The patient returned, later in the day. He told the doctor, "I had a very painful abscess, but I had to go and pray. And," he added, "after I'd prayed, the abscess burst. I'm already feeling much better."

Talking to me later, my friend said, "Perhaps his prayer was more effective than my medical treatment would've been!" At least the man had a clear idea of his priorities, and put prayer higher up the list than his personal comfort or convenience.

There's a thought for all of us.

And it was only at the end of the conversation that my friend added, "Oh, yes, one other thing . . . my patient was a Muslim."

Lord, judgement comes so easily to me.
To skim the surface of another's life.
To fasten on the bits that I don't understand
and use as evidence against him.
So easy to divide the world.
So satisfying too,
to crystallize the categories
into us and them.

If I can say he's wrong,
it strengthens my conviction
that I must be right.
Helps me to live a comfortable, comforting
exclusivity.
And adds a little hollow holiness
to my hypocrisy.

It's easier to judge than love.
Easier to pile up the differences,
brick on brick,
and build a wall.
To take the wall and build a house,
and live in it with judgement as companion,
love's presence elbowed out.
No room. No room.
Then chain the door,
drill through a little eyehole,
which offers me a small, constricted and distorted view
of what stands on the other side.

The trouble is,
that with each day that passes
it's harder to unlock the door
and ask love back.
And in the end
I'm left with judgement
when I could have lived with love.

Lord, help me hold prayer
as dear as he,
and leave the judgement
where it most belongs.
With you.
Although I have the feeling,
stronger every day,
that love will count the most.

Psalm 116:1-7

SOMETIME ago, my mother died. She was eighty-six years old, but it was sudden and a shock. We all felt the sadness.

A couple of days after her death, I went for a walk in the local nature reserve and down to the river. The peace and quiet were good, the light on the water beautiful. Then I passed a favourite group of alder trees I'd often sketched. There'd been some heavy windstorms, and rain. One of the trees had come down. The trunk lay in the dry winter grasses, the shattered stump showing raw, ragged edges.

I was sorry. I'd loved those trees. They'd never be the same again. Yet, walking on, I found some comfort in it. Not in its death, but in what it said to me. That death is part of the process of life. I don't want to argue with the theologians about our fallen world and how death came to be, but simply to say that we need to accept it as part of how things are. And whether it comes tragically and out of time, or quietly and in the fullness of years, we share the same vulnerability.

The vulnerability that Jesus took on himself as a human being, that saddened his family and friends. But a vulnerability that reminds and reassures me that he knows what it's all about, and knows how I feel.

The other trees will heal. Already the grass is beginning to grow. The wound will soften; still show, but mend.

I walked by the river, Lord,
after the storm.
Tall reeds, brown tips bent,
trailed fingers in the cold water.
I watched debris floating downstream.
Broken branches, planks,
and plastic bottles surfacing like ducks.
I skirted new falls of river bank,
raw fleshed, ragged, red like wounds.

But life was picking up its pieces.
The grasses shrugging off the wind,
stirring, straightening.
A kingfisher flashed neon-blue across the water,
sewing up the windtorn edges of the air.

But then I saw the stranded houseboat,
its stern well down below the water line,
broken bow high, mouth open for breath.

It was the human connection that hit me, Lord.
Reminded me of other storms
that gust hard in people's lives.
Winds that blow little good,
that warp, not reeds, but personality.

Life's river,
its surface broken by exhausted people
drifting helpless on the current.
Barely floating on the stream.
Hopes waterlogged.

Lord, the reeds, the river bank,
I leave to nature to repair.
The broken tree will heal,
send out new shoots.
Fresh-knitted grass soon covers
the earth's raw edges, purl and plain.

But the people, Lord?
In the noise of wind and stream
I hear you call.
Sometimes, your voice comes,
not from the safety of the river bank,
but from the middle of the stream.
Drawing me into its deepest part.

To risk, to rescue.
And sometimes I hear, distinctly,
that same voice from higher up the river.
Reminding me it's not enough
merely to offer help
to those already in the water.
You're asking me to make the river safe.

Lord, help me now
to think of all who struggle,
whose lives are flooded with care.
Help me to grasp each opportunity to help.
To change things in my world,
our world, your world.
And help them to recognize, however faintly,
that you are with them.
Swimming against the current.
Buoying them up.
Offering them the waters of life.

This meditation was originally published by The Mothers' Union, and is reprinted with their permission.

"The Secret Pool"

1 John 3:16-20

I HAVE seen the face of the planet Jupiter. It was craggy, apparently barren, unfamiliar. Like millions of other people, I watched it on television.

The American space probe Voyager 2 sent back clear and vivid pictures of the planet's surface. It had travelled more than three thousand million miles through space in a twelve year journey. It arrived only a few seconds late (I know church members who travel one mile and regularly arrive ten minutes late!) and only twenty miles from its projected arrival point, almost on the edge of the solar system.

The technology is awesome. To plan, build, and control a vehicle to that level of accuracy is an achievement that blows the mind.

Twenty years ago, I watched the first men ever to walk on the moon, the first significant step in exploring that part of the universe we call "ours". Now we've reached out to its limits, and Voyager has disappeared into the immensity of space beyond.

It leaves me spellbound but it also leaves me wondering. We can see the face of Jupiter but does it help us to see more clearly the face of our neighbour and his need? While we reach into space, people stay hungry, homeless, sick. Sometimes, for all the notice we take of them, they might live on a different planet. But they are here with us, now. How much technology do we need to reach out and touch them?

Lord, the camera shows me things
I never thought to see.
The wonders of your universe
brought close, before my eyes.
The sleight of hand of cosmic conjurers,
their science mathematical,
precise.
It's no small feat
to break out from the garden
you've given us on earth,
reach out,
and catch the stars.

But conscience is a casualty,
the rocket's roar
covering the cries of suffering.
The hunger,
printing pain on human faces,
unnoticed
as we trace trajectories across the screen.
The suffering's just another episode
in a television soap.
The hungry acting out a part
that loses impact
with each day's repeat.

Lord, help me see
that if technology can't cope
with your demands
for justice, mercy —
I won't mention love,
that's just too much to ask —
then something's wrong.
The need is here.
And reaching out beyond our world
won't help.
You ask me,
not to reach for stars
but just to walk
the harder journey
to my neighbour
down the road.

Matthew 6:19-24

SYDNEY Carter's song "Lord of the Dance" owes some of its inspiration to the Shakers. Its melody is based on a Shaker hymn tune, and perhaps even the thoughts began there.

The Shakers established religious communities through parts of the USA, mainly during the nineteenth century. They were given the name because of the dancing movements they used during worship. Some would call them eccentric, but they were idealistic, celibate, and hardworking. They valued neither money nor personal ownership. Perhaps that does seem eccentric today.

Life, work, and worship went together. "Put your hands to work and your heart to God," they said. Now, there's only one Shaker community left, at a place called Sabbath Day Lake, and it only has nine members.

Many were skilled craftsmen and women. Today, their early hand-made furniture is highly prized by collectors. It's beautiful, even elegant, in line; often light and delicate, but strong. Simply and honestly made, it reflects Shaker lifestyle. At a recent antiques auction, collectors paid enormous prices for chairs, a small table, a three-drawer chest, and a little wooden box.

I find it sad. Not sad when beauty and craftsmanship are recognized and valued, but sad that the dedication that produced it is ignored. The quality of the furniture is recognized, but not the quality of faith. The by-product is prized, but not the love and commitment that produced it. The simple furniture of a community dedicated to poverty is now scrambled for by the wealthy, and is shown off as a status symbol.

It would be good to think that the furniture might one day speak its own message about where true wealth lies, and say something to its new owners about lifestyle.

Easy to say, Lord,
hands to work and hearts to God.

It sounds good.
Has a ring to it.
A fine phrase for my notebook,
written down and filed,
like so many others.
Instant aspiration,
acknowledged and instantly forgotten.
Good for a sermon, harder to live.

Lord, help me to live out what I say.
Help me to shape my life with honesty.
To plane it true.
Dovetail it with care
so that it holds together, strong and firm.
Not falling apart at the first knock,
like a home-made drawer.

And bless me, Lord,
that people, looking at my life,
may see your loving craftsmanship
in every part.

Sometimes I'm tempted
to take the easy way.
To skip the care,
to pack and bodge,
and just pretend
rough edges aren't important.
And won't be noticed with a casual glance.

When moments like that come,
then help me, Lord, to hold to you,
accept your standards of design.
To see that lines of beauty
spring from patient workmanship,
without short cuts.

Lord, take me, hands and heart.
Repair, restore, renew.

And take my life,
and polish it with joy.

Matthew 13:10-16

A BLIND man described the different sounds rain makes. One wet day, he'd stepped out of the house into the garden, and stood and listened.

He heard the patter of raindrops on the shrubbery, and a softer sound as the rain fell on the wet earth of the lawn. Falling on the gravel of the path it sounded harsher, more staccato, and gave yet a different sound as it hit the tiles and ran down the slope of the roof. Dripping from a leaky guttering, it splashed persistently on a stone, with a regular beat.

"I hadn't realized how different the sounds could be until then," he said.

It left me wondering about the different ways we "hear" God. Perhaps our perception and experience of him depend on the way we listen and use our other senses.

Some perceive God as a loving, comforting father, the one they turn to for reassurance and decision. Others experience him as a challenging, uncomfortable presence, disturbing them with new thoughts, taking them in directions they don't fully understand. Others perhaps hear him as a steady dripping of water on a stone, asking a response.

Some people don't hear him at all, and assume he's not there, when it's really the noise of their other priorities that drowns his voice.

Perhaps we hear him differently because our personalities and needs are different. Arguments about how God speaks to us, how we experience him, are as futile as disagreeing about the way we hear rain, and how it sounds. Surely, there isn't a "right" way to hear rain. It all depends where we stand, and how we listen.

And beyond the differing sounds, it's good to recognize that though the rain falls differently at different times, and whether it falls gently or heavily as shower or storm, essentially it renews life, encourages growth, brings fruit.

Lord, in the quietness
reach out and hold me.
Draw me gently into your peace.
And in the loving silence at your heart,
attune my ears
to hear the sounds I never listen to.

The harmony that lies in you,
the discords in the world you've put me in.
The laughter and the tears
in other people's lives.

Make me more sensitive to others' needs.
Sometimes, I hear the words
that others speak,
but fail to grasp their meaning.
Help me to hear the worry
hidden in a throw-away remark,
the fear wrapped in a joke,
the insecurity behind unbending dogmatism.
Let me identify the cry for help
so casually expressed.

Help me to listen more,
and think, and think,
before I speak,
and then to think again.

And, Lord, teach me
to hear sincerity
in those who see and say things
in a different way.
Give me the grace
not to condemn or criticize,
but first to search for common ground,
and grasp the things
that draw us all together,
not concentrate on what holds us apart.
Help me to take the richness
of another's thought,
and hold it,
precious as my own.

Above all, may I hear
the gentle echoes of your love,
reflected all around me.

Give me the joy
of listening to your voice,
the quiet rustle as your arms
enfold me.

Matthew 5:9

TWO or three days before the Gulf War began, with the bombing of military targets in Iraq, a major British newspaper printed a headline on its financial page.

"Where to invest if it's war in the Gulf."

With the prospect of people dying — young and old, military and civilian — protecting your money and, if possible, making a profit, seemed to be important. I almost wrote "making a killing" as the financial experts say.

We live in a sick society. We appear to learn little from the past. Western countries, and others, go on making weapons and looking for markets for them. I've never understood the logic of selling guns to other countries with the hope that they'll never use them. Or that it's alright as long as they don't use them on us. But then, maybe I'm just not clever enough.

It's a logic mothered and fathered by irresponsibility and greed. And now young men and women have to fight to rescue us from a position we helped to create.

"Blessed are the peacemakers," said Jesus. That doesn't just mean those who sit round the conference tables after the shooting war is over, or even try to nip it in the bud once it's begun. It has to mean those who look ahead and try to see tomorrow's consequences in today's actions. Not those who try to rescue peace from the carnage, but those who help create it in advance by right action.

And right action is another name for love. Charity begins at home. Pray God it doesn't stop there.

It wasn't my fault, Lord.
I said it many times
when I was small.
"The plate broke on its own."
"The milk spilt by itself," I'd say,
my eyes wide held in simulated innocence,
so quickly learned.

It's harder now, Lord,
since I've grown.
Harder to escape responsibility.
Yet still I try.
Still wrapped in self-deluding innocence,
I look around for cause,
and find it,
deep in others,
and never in myself.
I stand with Pilate,
washing my hands of guilt,
and leaving it with others.

But self-righteousness is risky,
a slippery slope
that sends me sprawling on my back
each time I try to stand on dignity.
I never seem to try
the firmer footing of humility.

Lord, help me see
that war and peace
begin with me.
No use my public cries,
my protest banners waving in the air,
if by my own indifference to others' needs
I help create injustice.

No use to put a flower in the rifle muzzle
which I have helped to make.

Acts 17:1-6

THE Bible story tells us that God drove Adam and Eve out of the garden because they disobeyed him. They were driven out into the world through disobedience. And, over the years of the Christian faith, "being worldly" has become a synonym for disobedience.

Many believers have drawn in their horizons and disengaged from the world to seek a spirituality and purity in a voluntary segregation. But Jesus Christ has changed the old prohibitions, turned them on their heads, and Christians are driven out into that same world because they choose to obey, rather than disobey.

We are driven into the world through obedience, following his call to be witnesses. Living, working, identifying, suffering with those who suffer. Bringing word of the beginning of a new world from which the old guilt has been removed, and in which all things are being renewed.

When a mob caught a group of early believers and hauled them before the civil authorities, they accused them of ". . . turning the world upside down," as the Authorized Version puts it.

That's what we're called to do. To change values and perceptions, overturn prejudice. To break out to freedom. To share in the creation of a new world of love within the old and suffering world of Adam. And we can do it only by being in it, as part of God's purposes.

I'm not quite sure if I should thank you, Lord,
or register objection.
Turning the world upside down
is not the first thing on my list of things to do.
It comes a bit below
concern for health and safety,
time off, holidays.
It's not a popular thing.
People object.
They like things as they are.

And so do I.
I like my life to be a steady progress,
comfortable, the pace sedate.
Looking before each little step,
no thought of leaps.

And when I've done my quota for the day,
I like to shut up shop,
go home. Relax.
Turn up the heating,
switch the telly on,
ignore the phone
and hope the cry for help
was just another double glazing salesman.
"I'm not available just now,
but if you leave your name and message
I'll get back to you as soon as it's convenient."

Convenient to me of course,
but that's just what you're not — convenient.
The least convenient God I could imagine.
Scrapping my carefully planned agenda.
Calling me to change the world.
To turn it upside down.

It seems too big a job for me,
and so it is,
except I'm not alone.
I've got you in my life.
And if it still seems hard
to change the world,
even with you,
perhaps, together, we can make a start
at changing me.

Psalm 23

I REMEMBER hearing a surgeon talk about his work among Afghan rebels during the Soviet occupation of their country. "There'll always be wars . . ." he said, ". . . over religion and politics . . . All I can do is make life a little better for a few individuals."

He seemed disillusioned and disappointed at the way we humans continue to accept force as a fact of life, and felt powerless to do more than help a few of the injured. At least he had helped, at some personal risk, using his gifts in a very positive way. Thank God for him.

His words came back to me as I watched "Songs of Praise" on television, on the first Sunday of the Gulf War. It came from Westminster Abbey. During the service, three people shared in the reading of Psalm 23 — a Jewish rabbi, a Muslim priest, and a Christian. All three faiths value the psalm as part of their traditions. The rabbi read in Hebrew, the Muslim in Arabic, the Christian in English. In each language the psalm acknowledges God's goodness and love, and looks to him for guidance.

The presence of these representatives was, I hope and believe, a confession that war is always a failure of understanding and compassion, and that if we looked deeper we would find things to unite rather than divide us. Perhaps sitting in the presence of our enemies around the table God prepares for us would help.

Some sincere Christians, and I suppose Muslims and Jews too, will feel uneasy at the three faiths being brought together for prayer in a Christian church. I know the stock questions and answers, but can any joint prayer for peace be wrong?

There are things that separate us, matters of doctrine and belief, but refusing to pray together, refusing to talk together, begins to sow the seeds of the next conflict. Begins to make more work for the surgeon, continues the lack of understanding, produces more grief and tears.

Perhaps if we all followed the surgeon, and tried "to make life a little better for a few individuals", things might begin to change.

Lord, I sometimes wonder
why you don't give up on us.
Shepherding, surely, should never be this hard.
We take the freedom that you've given us,
nurtured so lovingly,
and use it to rebel.

You'd think the still waters of your presence,
the gift of green pastures, would be enough.
But it only takes one sheep
to get a stubborn thought and make a run for it,
and we all follow in a flock.
Crash headlong through the hedge of love
you put there for our safety.
Run bleating into trouble.

Not my fault, Lord, we say.
I'm not to blame for anything.
The other man began it all.
The war's not of my choosing.
So easy, somehow, to ignore
all that we've done — or not done —
to create the discontent, provoke the anger,
feed the acid hatred
that etches violence on the plate of life.

And when we spoil life's image,
see no way out,
we lay the blame on you.
We ask "Why does God let it happen?"

That must be hard, Lord,
to see your loving kindness
thrown back at you in glib hypocrisy.
And yet the wonder is you don't give up.
Your love goes on through everyone
who tries to make this world a better place.
Your spirit's compassion
nudging us nearer to understanding,
showing us the possibility
and joy of reconciliation.

And, one day, Lord,
when we are more amenable,
perhaps we'll find a way of fellowship.
To sit together at your table

in the presence of the friends whom we made enemies.
And when we reach the valley of the shadow
we'll walk through it together.
Instead of pushing someone else ahead.

It's down to us, Lord, now.
You've pointed out the way.

"Going Home for Tea"

Psalm 98:4-9

SOME North American Indians hold a legend. It says that when the Great Spirit created the world, he also created a song. He gave a piece of that song to each part of creation, a part to the trees, a part to rocks, to animals, to humankind. The song, they say, is only complete when everything sings together.

They see themselves as part of creation, part of the song. They respect the earth, but don't believe they own it. They are part of it, part of all that God has made, everything and everyone linked in a mutual dependency.

I hear echoes of the Psalmist, who holds a vision of the whole earth full of jubilant music. The mountains singing for joy at God's righteousness, the sea echoing it, the rivers full of applause. Humanity joins in, shouting for joy. What a symphony!

Although the North American Indians had never heard the word, theirs was a picture of shalom. That wonderful harmony which God created, the dynamic balance of relationships between humanity and the world in which we live, between humans themselves, and between us and God.

Their dream was damaged cruelly in the struggle with Europeans which lasted well into this century. Perhaps it's still not resolved. A struggle between "savages" who had the humility to see themselves as responsible to creation, and the "civilized" who believed their power and knowledge gave them the right to take whatever they wanted, with little thought for the consequences.

Today, perhaps, we're moving nearer to that "primitive" philosophy and beginning to realize that the only way to save the earth and its resources is to acknowledge that it's a trust to be treasured, rather than a storehouse to be plundered.

And if that humility roots deeper into our relationships, we'll hear that joyful song again, as we join in praise of the creator.

A last thought: I said the Indians had never heard the word shalom. Maybe that comment itself is part of our unconscious arrogance. They may not have heard it in Hebrew, but I believe they'd felt it in their bones, and that it was a feeling God had planted.

Lord, I want to sing your song.
A song of joy.
Want to respond to all you've done.
But my small voice
gets drowned in sounds of selfishness.

The earth too, your earth, no longer sings.
The hurt sea moans its disillusion.
The mountains scream in pain.
The rivers lift their hands to clap,
but the sound is lost,
its echoes dying in the distance.
The old song drops notes like dead petals
browned by the sudden frost of my indifference.

And when I hear some scrap of music from your world,
it's in a minor key.
Sad song of sorrow for lost innocence.
The harmony's gone,
and life's discords set my teeth on edge.
Not music, more the scratching of a fingernail
across a blackboard.

And, lest I seem to be the only one in step,
I must admit my own complicity.
The selfishness that's mine.
It's easier to share the spoils
than stand for righteousness.

Yet still you sing your song.
A melody of love and grace, and infinite patience.
A harmony of hope, striking chords
which pull my heart gently
in your direction.

Keep singing, Lord,
and, in my little way, let me join in.
Renewed with all the earth
in praise at what you are,
and what is still to come.
And if there's yet
an undertone of sadness in the song
for all that's gone before,
it counterpoints the joy,
enriches harmony.

Index